TRESCO
ABBEY GARDEN

—————— *The Garden Guide* ——————

Published by Truran

Truran is an imprint of Tor Mark Ltd,
United Downs Industrial Estate,
St Day, Redruth, Cornwall TR16 5HY

www.tormark.co.uk

First published 2007, reprinted 2008, 2011, 2016
Second edition 2019, this reprint 2021

ISBN 978 1 85022 212 5

Text © Mike Nelhams, 2007, 2008, 2011, 2019

Images © Adobe 2019, © As listed, © Clive Nichols,
© Mike Nelhams, © Shutterstock, © Tresco Estate

Map © Alix Wood

Front cover image: The Shell House © Clive Nichols
Reverse front cover image: The Old Abbey © Emily Luxton
Reverse back cover image: The Middle Terrace © Clive Nichols

THE HISTORY OF TRESCO

Tresco Garden was created early in the nineteenth century by Augustus Smith. He had taken over the lease of all of the islands from the Duchy of Cornwall in 1834. A man of independent means and an equally independent spirit, the seclusion of Tresco suited him admirably.

He realised that the islands were blessed with a wonderfully mild climate - the shores washed by the Gulf Stream ensuring a virtually frost-free environment where he could create an exotic garden unlike anything on mainland Britain.

A thousand years earlier a Benedictine priory had been established but very little remained. A couple of archways and some broken down walls but it was enough to catch Smith's imagination. The islands, though blessed with this mild climate, were lashed by the salt-laden Atlantic gales and he realised that a priority was to create shelter belts to protect his new Garden. He quickly found two trees that were both salt-tolerant and quick growing, the *Monterey Pine* and *Cypress*, both from California.

Neptune statue

He cleverly used the indigenous gorse to protect the young saplings.

As the shelter belt grew so did the Garden, and Smith's horticultural knowledge, so that in time he was recognised as a considerable plantsman. This allowed him to correspond with other influential gardeners including Sir William Hooker at Kew Gardens. This relationship was especially fruitful and the Abbey Garden and plant collection developed rapidly.

It has been particularly fortunate that the Garden has been in the care of the same family for five generations. This has given continuity and commitment. Each generation has made its contribution. Despite the benign weather there have been a number of climatic disasters; the first in December 1929 when a five day storm destroyed 600 mature trees including much of the shelter belt. More recently in our own time the great snows of 1987 and the hurricane of 1990 caused immense damage especially one coming immediately after the other.

On each occasion the Garden has been restored, replanted and re-planned. This was only made possible by the dedication of the gardeners and the owners. In addition, plants were 'borrowed' from other gardens - it cannot be overemphasised how important this informal networking of gardeners throughout the country is for the preservation and development of all major gardens.

From early on visitors were encouraged, initially slipping the head gardener half a crown and later in the twentieth century, visitors were asked to make a voluntary donation. By the late 1950s numbers were in excess of seventeen thousand and it was agreed that an admission charge would have to be applied to ensure sufficient income to maintain and develop the Garden.

Augustus Smith in his Masonic regalia

Augustus Smith in 1861 with the estate workers outside his house

© Jules Rowe

Valhalla, built by Augustus Smith to house his collection of figurehe

© Jim Richardson

© Povl Abrahamsen

As well as being interested in the welfare of the islands and in developing his Garden, Augustus Smith began a collection of figureheads and other artefacts from the many wrecks around the islands. At first the collection was on the Abbey terrace, but later around 1870 a purpose-built home was created.

Figureheads are carvings fixed to the bows of ships as decoration; their purpose and meaning is not clear, but they are beautiful and evocative objects - a sad reminder of ships and lives lost. There are 28 figureheads in the Valhalla collection, coming from the latter half of the nineteenth century from merchant sailing and steamship vessels. Within the collection are also name boards, decorative stern boards, lifebuoys, anchors, a pair of brass signal guns from the terrible passenger ship disaster of the *Schiller* in 1875, and a handsome bronze gun from the wreck of the *Association*, which went down in 1707.

A new addition at the Visitor Centre is the iconic 3.3m tall wood stern carving from the wreck of HMS *Colossus*, 1793.

© Alistair Young

Figurehead from the *Palinurus* (34) wrecked off St Martin's in 1848 - all the 17 crew were drowned

Figurehead from the *Serica* (5) wrecked in 1893, south west of St Mary's

THE MEDITERRANEAN GARDEN

Passing over the blue entrance bridge, you enter through the most recently developed part of the Garden. The vista before you runs up to a crossroads and onwards and upwards through the bronze archway towards the *Agave* fountain in the Mediterranean Garden. Immediately you are aware that this is not a typical English garden. All around you are *Proteas*, *Aloes*, *Cordyline*, *Silver Trees* and *Dasylirion* - plants of an altogether different and exotic world.

Walking through the archway will take you across the shaded long walk and up towards the splendid garden water sculpture by local Cornish artist, Tom Leaper based on the North American 'Century Plant', flanked by two *Canary Island Palms*. Passing by clipped Olive Trees up a series of steps to the Olive Terrace with distinctive purple *Aeonium* and a view out to the ocean and the island of Samson. This close relationship with the sea is so important to the character of the Garden.

© Povl Abrahamsen

The Mediterranean Garden developed in 1991
© Clive Nichols

© Rob Dawson

© Rob Dawson

The Robinson Crusoe
cabbage tree

THE LONG WALK

The Long Walk is easily recognised as it is the only straight pathway running the full length of the Garden. It is believed to be the first significant development extending the Garden beyond the Old Abbey ruins. The path is at the bottom of the south-facing hillside; in consequence the soil is deep which has allowed many larger mature trees to grow.

In time, this has created more shade and better water retention which allows for the growth of plants that would normally require higher rainfall than experienced on Tresco. These include a number of plants from New Zealand and the Canary Islands. The giant *Metrosideros excelsa* or *'Pohutukawa'* give shade to *Rhopalostylis* palms and *Dicksonia* and *Cyathea*, the tree ferns, *Brachyglottis*, *Nothofagus*, *Pseudopanax*, *Agathis*, *Meryta* and *Macropiper excelsa* (Pepper Tree), which are all native to the forests of New Zealand.

In the spring months *Sonchus arboreus*, (Tree Dandelion) will grow to a height of four metres, its long slender leaves topped by bright yellow flowers on stalks.

Nearby the giant multi-stemmed trunks of *Eucalyptus globulus*, (Tasmanian Blue Gum) stand out in rain or shine.

Dense plantings of flowering plants such as *Canna*, *Hedychium* and *Musa* punctuate the green carpets of undergrowth and occasional 'sunny windows' allow shafts of light and views to lawns, paths and terraces as one walks along towards the western end where you can see the Roman altar.

Top left image: *Sonchus arboreus* (Tree Dandelion)
Bottom left image: The Long Walk Pathway
Right image: The *Rhopalostylis* palm - the *Nikau* palm

THE NEPTUNE STEPS

Standing with the *Tresco Children* sculpture behind and looking up, you will see the imposing thirty foot tall evergreen oak, *Quercus ilex* hedges that have been holding back salt-laden Atlantic gales for over a hundred years. Looking through these living walls of green is a view unrivalled in any British garden.

Sitting at the top of the steps astride a granite plinth is the stone-like figure of 'Neptune' which has looked down upon the Garden since 1841. In fact this is a ship's figurehead from the *SS Thames* a steam-ship wrecked upon the Western Rocks. Lower down on the Middle Terrace are the magnificent specimens of *Phoenix canariensis*, (Canary Island Palm) which dominate the heart of the Garden from almost every angle.

The steps chiselled from island granite run down the south-facing hillside adorned with clay pots designed by Augustus Smith. At your feet the path is edged by the ubiquitous spider plant, *Chloropythum comosum*. From here you can see plants from all corners of the world, notably *Luma apiculata* from Chile with its distinctive brown trunk which stands out particularly in August when the tree is laden with white scented flowers and covered in bees; *Coleonema album* with its scented foliage and large clusters of succulent plants; *Aloe, Mesembryanthemum, Rochea* - all from South Africa - and a variety of *Aeonium* from the Canary Islands. As you ascend you will glimpse David Wynne's *Gaia*, Mother Earth.

Tresco Children by David Wynne

Richard Guy

THE OLD ABBEY

The area surrounding the Old Abbey ruin is important because it was here that Augustus Smith made his first landscaped planting. It is believed Benedictine monks settled here between 1042 and 1066. The priory is dedicated to St Nicholas and is mentioned in a charter of 1120 in the time of Henry I. The wall surrounding the ruins also takes in the Pebble Garden and leads off into the Well Garden where it is thought the monks discovered water.

Many palm trees are represented in and around this area. *Phoenix canariensis* from the Canary Isles, *Washingtonia filifera* from California, *Cordyline australis* from New Zealand, *Livistonia australis* (Fountain Palm) from Australia and most impressive of all *Jubea spectabilis* (Chilean Wine Palm) with its barrel-like trunk which comes from the mountains of Chile.

Here too are large specimens of *Doryanthes excelsa* (Queensland Lily) which has leaves three metres long and extravagant red flowers on stems five metres tall, which bloom in late spring.

Directly below the Pebble Garden is a bed containing many different and fragrant leafed *Salvia* plants and the large leafed *Wigandia urens* collected from the famous Hanbury Garden in Italy.

Chamaerops excelsa

© Rob Dawson

Beschorneria flower

THE MIDDLE TERRACE

The Middle Terrace is the heart of the Garden. By starting at the West Rockery, below the house built by Augustus Smith, you will see Australian *Banksia*, South African *Pelargonium* and Canary Island *Cytissus* all clinging to a rockery and flanked by monumental hedges of *Quercus ilex* (Evergreen Oak). Moving through the archway to the right will bring you to a sloping bank of *Fascicularia* and *Ochagavia* bushes with brightly coloured leaf bracts and by looking down you will see the Pebble Garden in the design of a Union Jack flag, where the Garden was first landscaped.

The quarry-like cliff cut into the bedrock has succulent plants from all regions of the world: *Aloe arborescens*, which flowers with flame-red spikes at Christmas, *Aeonium*, both green and purple, with yellow flowers in June, brightly coloured *Mesembryanthemum* hanging in large clusters from small soil pockets and *Oscularia* with its pink flowers in large sheets hanging down like a carpet.

Standing at the Neptune Steps crossway and looking across the Garden, you would be forgiven for thinking you had been dropped into some far-flung botanical paradise. Walking along the terrace and past the fishponds and summerhouse decorated with the unusual elephant and fist family crest, colourful banks of mixed exotica are crowded together for spectacular effect: *Echium*, *Watsonia*, *Arctotis*, *Gazania*, *Agave*, *Puya* and *Passiflora* all fight for position in what is the most sheltered and most exuberant part of the Garden.

Aloe polyphylla

Echium x scilloniensis

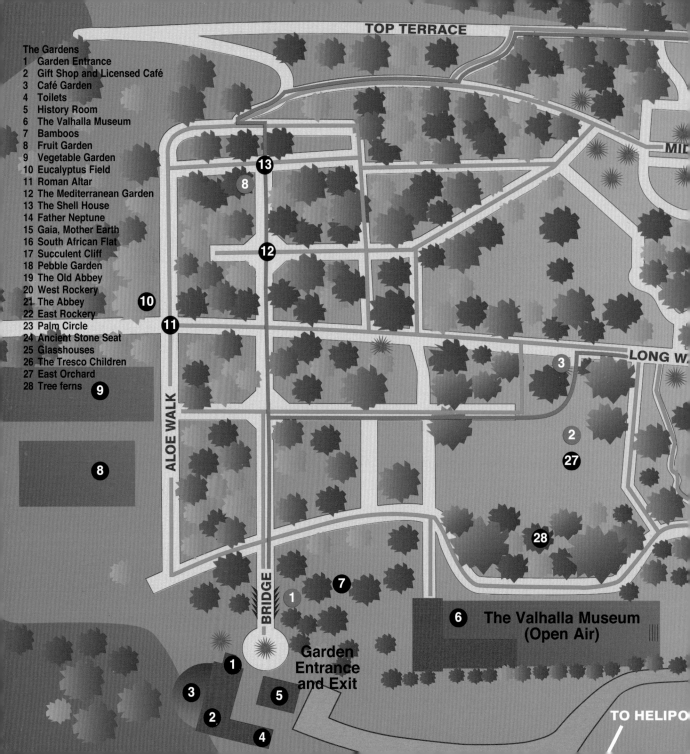

The Gardens
1 Garden Entrance
2 Gift Shop and Licensed Café
3 Café Garden
4 Toilets
5 History Room
6 The Valhalla Museum
7 Bamboos
8 Fruit Garden
9 Vegetable Garden
10 Eucalyptus Field
11 Roman Altar
12 The Mediterranean Garden
13 The Shell House
14 Father Neptune
15 Gaia, Mother Earth
16 South African Flat
17 Succulent Cliff
18 Pebble Garden
19 The Old Abbey
20 West Rockery
21 The Abbey
22 East Rockery
23 Palm Circle
24 Ancient Stone Seat
25 Glasshouses
26 The Tresco Children
27 East Orchard
28 Tree ferns

TOP TERRACE

MID

LONG WA

ALOE WALK

BRIDGE

Garden
Entrance
and Exit

6 The Valhalla Museum
(Open Air)

TO HELIPO

TO NEW GRIMSBY

7 14

17

16

15 NEPTUNE STEPS

RRACE

6

18

19 Old Abbey

5

4

21 (Private)

22

20

23

LIGHTHOUSE WALK

25 24

OAD OUTSIDE THE GARDEN

wheelchair and scooter friendly

The Quick Tour
1 Blue Bridge
2 East Orchard
3 Long Walk
4 Vista to Neptune Steps
5 Towards Pebble Garden
6 Middle Terrace
7 Top Terrace
8 Shell House

View over the Old Abbey from the Top Terrace
© Clive Nichols

THE TOP TERRACE

Looking down from the highest point in the Garden and out to sea, the Top Terrace reflects the hot dry conditions of South Africa and Australia. The soils are free draining, poor in nutrient and the conditions windy with high light levels.

This is perfect for the many *Proteaceae* family that grow here with species such as *Banksia*, *Dryandra*, *Leucadendron*, *Leucospermum*, *Grevillea*, *Telopea*, *Hakea*, *Isopogon* and of course *Protea*.

The Pincushion plant - *Leucospermum cordifolium*

Watsonia - 'Tresco hybrid'

At the eastern end of the terrace you look down upon the Old Abbey, the Pebble Garden and out over the sea to the islands of St Mary's and St Agnes. From here *Banksia grandis* from Australia is prominent when in flower in the spring with candle-like yellow flowers up to half a metre high.

Moving past the *SS Thames* figurehead will bring you along to borders filled with a variety of *Aloe*, *Aeonium*, and assorted succulents. As you move along towards the western end *Cape Heathers*, *Cistus* and *Callistemon* all flourish alongside *Telopea speciosissima* with its flowers standing out like beacons in the surrounding vegetation.

THE ABBEY HILL

Protecting the Garden on the north and west sides sits Abbey Hill. Although not formally part of the Garden it has great importance in providing shelter from the severe Atlantic salt-laden gales that can lash across the island in the winter months. This shelter belt was planted with quick-growing and salt-tolerant pines in 1874 and again in 1894.

Since then many other woodland trees have joined them. From the Southern Hemisphere *Eucalyptus* and *Leptospermum* have freely seeded themselves along with numerous *Acacia* species which flower from early January up to late May notably *Acacia longifolia*, *Acacia verticillata* and *Acacia melanoxylon*. A native to the forests of Madeira *Clethra arborea* (Lily of the Valley Tree) grows to a height of twenty metres and produces creamy white scented flowers in September.

Of all of Tresco's exotics, probably the most wind tolerant, is the giant *Metrosideros excelsa* (Pohutukawa) from New Zealand. An evergreen, it has bright red flowers in July and is known as the Ironwood due to the hardness of its wood. Without the protection of these large woodland trees, the Garden would not be able to grow the wide range of plants that come from the diverse, Mediterranean climates of the world.

Sparmannia Africana

Acacia longifolia

PLANTS FROM SOUTH AFRICA

Plants from the Western Cape of South Africa are very well represented within the Abbey Garden. The nutrient-free soil conditions allied to a free draining, sunny and breezy aspect make the perfect spot to show a wide and varied collection. In the winter months over sixty varying *Aloe* species flower between December and March on Tresco representing the spring and summer season of the Cape. *Cape Heathers* in many different forms will delight the garden visitor with an abundant array of colourful tubes and trumpets. Succulent *Mesembryanthemum*, *Oscularia* and *Drosanthemum* cling to hot dry slopes, all growing bright, highly coloured and visible flowers in full sun, making a most spectacular display.

Many *Protea* species such as *Protea cynaroides* (King Protea), grow like weeds whilst *Leucadendron argenteum* will thrive in a frost-free environment outdoors as nowhere else in Britain. The *Strelitzia reginae* (Bird of Paradise plant) is instantly recognisable with its humming bird-like flower.

Here *Watsonia* 'Tresco Hybrid' from the family *Iridaceae* produces sweeping drifts of brightly coloured stems in August.

All these plants will respond to the dry hot summers and mild wet winters typical of both South Africa and the Isles of Scilly.

South African Aloe

Top left image: *Protea neriifolia*
Bottom left image: *Strelitzia reginae* - Bird of Paradise
Top right image: *Agapanthus orientalis x africanus*
Bottom right image: *Mesembryanthemum*

PLANTS FROM AUSTRALIA

The vegetation of Australia is particularly noted for its richness of species, approximately 15,000, of which 8,000 come from a small number of families. There are two Mediterranean climate areas in Australia, one in Western and another in South Australia.

Most prominent are the *Acacia* (Wattle) trees which belong to the *Pea* family and are among the world's largest families with about 1,200 species. They typically bear yellow, puffy flowers.

Corymbia ficifolia

The *Myrtle* family is characterized by trees and shrubs with aromatic leaves and within this group are found *Eucalyptus*, *Kunzea*, *Melaleuca* (Paper Bark Tree) with its many layers of paper thin tissue bark and the very recognisable *Callistemon* otherwise known as 'Bottlebrush'.

Banksia integrifolia

The *Protea* family is as prominent in Australia as it is in the Western Cape of South Africa, *Banksia* being the best known, with its large cylindrical flowers. Other large genera within *Proteaceae* include *Grevillea*, *Hakea* and *Dryandra*. Smaller shrubs provide a lot of colour such as the *Correa* which was introduced into Europe in the early 19th century.

Top left image: *Telopea speciosissima*
Bottom left image: *Callistemon citrinus splendens*
Right image: *Leptospermum scoparium*

© Jo O'Callaghan

© Jo O'Callaghan

© Jo O'Callagh

— PLANTS FROM CALIFORNIA AND MEXICO —

Two important trees that form the shelter belt planting surrounding the Abbey Garden are *Pinus radiata* (Monterey Pine) and *Cupressus macrocarpa* (Monterey Cypress), both native of the Monterey peninsula in California. Without these fast-growing, salt-tolerant trees the Garden would not have developed so quickly or been able to allow such a variety of plants to flourish.

Monterey pine reaches an average height of 25 metres and its trunk is red-brown and deeply furrowed. Cones of the Monterey pine remain tightly closed until the heat from a fire or an exceptionally hot day opens them. Californian *Ceonothus* will also be familiar to many garden visitors across the world with its distinctive blue flowers.

From Mexico comes the *Agave* (Century Plant) which stands out in any garden with a bold striking shape. The majority of the species will flower only once in their lives then die, but not before producing a flower-spike that grows very quickly sometimes up to 7 metres.

Also from Mexico in the same vein come *Dasylirion, Yucca whipplei* and *Furcraea longeava* which all produce impressive fast-growing flower spikes. Small bulbs such as *Tigridia pavonia*, (Tiger Flower) provide a succession of summer flowers, each lasting for just one day.

Agave victoriae-reginae

Top left image: *Agave ferox*
Bottom left image: *Tigridia pavonia*
Top right image: *Yucca whipplei*
Bottom right image: *Agave americana variegate*

PLANTS FROM CHILE

The Mediterranean climate area of central Chile extends for about one third of the length of the country; its climate is strikingly similar to that of California with coastal ranges, central valleys and foothills running into mountains.

If you are interested in palms, then look no further than the barrel-trunked *Jubea chilensis* (Chilean Wine Palm). Once abundant in the valleys and lower slopes of the Chilean coastal ranges, plants were cut down for their abundant sap which flowed for months and was used to make palm honey. In the 17th and 18th centuries this was the major source of sugar for the entire country.

Puya chilensis © Jo O'Callaghan

From the *Bromeliad* family comes *Puya chilensis* (also called Chagual) which has a rosette of stiff, spiny leaves from the centre of which a flower stalk bearing bright yellow flowers rises to 3.5 metres. *Embothrium coccineum* (Chilean Firebush) is one of the more prominent flowering shrubs from the family *Proteaceae* and lives in the moister, southern part of central Chile.

The best known climber is *Lapageria rosea*, Chile's national flower. This striking deep red bell-shaped flower is pollinated by humming birds and flowers all year round on evergreen vines that climb up shrubs and trees.

Top left image: *Lapageria rosea*
Bottom left image: *Brugmansia sanguinea*
Top right image: *Abutilon vitifolium*
Bottom right image: *Fascicularia bicolor*

Cyathea medullaris and *Dicksonia antarctica* tree ferns
© Alistair Young

PLANTS FROM NEW ZEALAND

Strictly speaking New Zealand does not have a Mediterranean climate, but many of the native plants from there thrive in Mediterranean conditions. Although usually requiring a more humid atmosphere and a good deal more rain, many species flourish in the microclimate on Tresco, where there is also shade, shelter and deeper soil. Most of the plants are evergreen, often with large leaves and unshowy flower displays.

Looming large above all others is, *Metrosideros excelsa* (Pohutukawa tree). Growing best close to the sea in its natural habitat, it will produce massive spreading branches often smothered with crimson to bright-red flowers, which are a brilliant spectacle. Tree ferns include *Dicksonia* and *Cyathea medullaris* (Black Tree Fern) due to the colour of the trunk and new fronds.

The *Rhopalostylis sapida* (Nikau Palm) will reach a height of ten metres and has the distinction of being the most southerly naturally growing palm in the world. The *Pseudopanax* (Lancewoods) are a wide group of trees and shrubs that are very popular as garden plants with a varied foliage. *Xeronema*

callistemon with its long red poker like flowers shines out from the middle terrace in the summer months.

Xeronema callistemon

Sophora microphylla

PLANTS FROM THE CANARY ISLES

The mountains, forests and coasts of the Canary Islands and neighbouring Madeira, harbour a wealth of plants, of which a large proportion are peculiar to the archipelago. The climate is basically a Mediterranean one but influenced by close proximity to the coast of North Africa which means hot, dry summers and warm wet winters.

Instantly noticeable is the Canary Island Date Palm, *Phoenix canariensis*, a large spreading palm up to 20 metres high. Somewhat smaller are an assortment of *Echiums* ranging from the single tall deep blue flower spike of the, bi-annual *Echium pininiana*, contrasting with the pink *Echium wildpretti* to the multi-headed *Echium callithyrsum* and *Echium webbii*.

There are vibrant colours from plants such as *Cytissus proliferus*, *Argyranthemum frutescens* and the self-seeding *Geranium maderense* will be evident in the spring months. Small shrubs that catch the eye include *Sonchus arboreus* (Tree Dandelion), *Musschia wollastonii* from Madeira and *Isoplexus canariensis* with its striking orange flowers.

Succulents are well represented by the many self-seeding *Aeoniums*. Many species abound producing large central yellow summer flowers from a rosette of fleshy leaves. Probably the most showy and unusual being *Aeonium atropurpureum* a purple-leafed plant that contrasts strongly with the usual garden green.

Left image: *Geranium maderense*
Top right image: *Aeonium atropurpureum*
Bottom right image: *Echium x scilloniensis*

Phoenix Palm

Roger Nix

© Roger Nix

Tresco Abbey - the family home of the Dorrien-Smiths
© Chris Hurl

TRESCO ABBEY GARDEN

The Garden has been developed since 1834 by a continuous line of Dorrien-Smiths who have all been committed to the Garden and island. Now Robert and Lucy Dorrien-Smith continue to maintain the island for both family, islanders and visitors alike.

The Tresco Abbey Garden welcomes visitors from all over the world. The Garden employs nine gardeners, including Garden Curator Mike Nelhams and Head Gardener Andrew Lawson. Every year three Studley College Trust horticultural students spend twelve months working with the Garden team. The Garden has numerous contacts with other great gardens of the world for seed, plant and exchange of information.

The Garden is open every day of the year
www.tresco.co.uk

Protea cynaroides - King Protea © Clive Nichols

Pincushion plant © Jo O'Callaghan

BOOKS ABOUT TRESCO
Ronald King; *Tresco Island of Flowers, 1985, Constable*
Elisabeth Inglis-Jones; *Augustus Smith of Scilly, 1969, Faber and Faber*
Sam Llewellyn; *Emperor Smith - The Man who Built Scilly, 2005, Dovecote Press*
Mike Nelhams; *Tresco Abbey Garden - a personal and pictorial history, 2000, Truran*

A QUICK TOUR AROUND THE GARDEN

Cross the blue bridge at the Garden entrance and walk to the crossroads with the blue benches. Here you can see a collection of plants from all of the Mediterranean climate zones; the *Proteas* from South Africa, the *Agaves* from Mexico, the *Cordyline indivisa* from New Zealand, the *Aeonium* from the Canary Islands and the *Callistemon* from Australia.

2

Bear right and the path opens out into the East Orchard where there is a grove of Norfolk Island pines on the right and the ancient and newly rediscovered *Wollemi Pine* in the middle.

Norfolk Island Pine

Wollemi Pine

Pass through an opening on the left onto the middle of the Long Walk (page 13). Along this shady walk are a number of plants from New Zealand and the Canary Islands. On the left you see a fabulous *Eucalyptus* and the *Rhopalostylis sapida* palm tree.

Stop to look at the crossroads at the Vista up the Neptune Steps (page 14) and on the right the statue, *Tresco Children*. Continue past a grove of tree ferns on the right just after the crossroads and walk to the end turning left up some steps to discover the remains of the Old Abbey (page 19).

Tresco Children

Turn left just before the arch, - although a minor diversion into the Old Abbey ruins is a good idea - then turn right up the steps and immediately left to the Pebble Garden, dominated by the magnificent *Butia capitata* palm from Brazil. Move up through the Union Jack-shaped Pebble Garden - first made in Augustus Smith's time - to the top left hand corner. Go through the arbour to the Middle Terrace (page 22). Turn left.

The Middle Terrace is the heart of the Garden with the cliff abounding in *Aloes* and *Aeonium*. Pass a huge *Agave* and some Canary Island Palms which have now become a symbol of Tresco. When you get to the Neptune Steps turn right and go up them, between two silver trees - *Leucadendron argentum* - at the top.

A QUICK TOUR AROUND THE GARDEN

Now you are on the Top Terrace (page 27) where you have views across the sea to St Mary's, St Agnes and Samson. Going left along the Terrace take a left fork downhill, passing banks of South African *Aloes*. At the T-junction turn right, pass the huge *Monterey Cypress* and you are directly above the Mediterranean Garden (page 8). Go down the steps.

Here is the Shell House, decorated by Lucy Dorrien-Smith (page 11). As you walk down through the Garden you pass Olive Trees and purple *Aeoniums*. There is the lovely *Agave* fountain. Keep straight on and over the blue bridge back to the visitor centre. If you have time follow the sign to take a look at Valhalla (page 7).

The Shell House © Michael Day

Valhalla

www.tormark.co.uk